A guide to writing a résumé,
crafting a cover letter,
owning an interview, and
accepting a job offer.

Your

Job

Search

Résumés,
Interviews, and
More

Laura M. LaVoie

Your Job Search: Résumés, Interviews, and More

By Laura M. LaVoie

Laura M. LaVoie is a freelance writer living in the mountains of western North Carolina. Before writing full time, Laura worked for 15 years as a recruiter for the temporary staffing industry. She has read and reviewed thousands of résumés and conducted just as many interviews. This book is a beginner's guide to a successful job search.

Also by Laura M. LaVoie

120 Ideas for Tiny Living

How to Drink Craft Beer: A Beginner's Guide

Disclaimer

Finding the right job for you is about hard work and persistence. The tips presented in this guide are intended to help you polish your job search and find your next opportunity. Unfortunately, no one can guarantee employment, and the author can't claim responsibility for the success or failure of your search.

Introduction

One of the biggest complaints I heard while I worked as a recruiter is that no one was ever actually taught how to write a résumé and interview for a job. Everyone is just expected to have these abilities. I also saw that candidates who chose to "wing" their job search rarely had success and quickly became jaded and angry about the process.

After spending 15 years in staffing, I saw innumerable résumés, and some of them were, in fact, exceptional. However, most had easy-to-fix mistakes or other issues which likely contributed to the barriers between seekers and jobs.

Candidates also viewed interviews as one of the most terrifying prospects of their professional lives. While many hiring managers are also unskilled at interviewing techniques, it is important for the job seeker to feel confident during these meetings and to put their best foot forward. It isn't up to the employer to do it right.

Finally, a little advice will help someone in their job search if they are uncomfortable with checking back in with the potential employer the right way. By following the sections in this book, you can feel a little more confident about your approach, you will be able to tailor a résumé to your needs and those of the hiring company, and you will feel more prepared to discuss your experience in an interview.

Table of Contents

How to Write a Résumé

"One important key to success is self-confidence. An important key to self-confidence is preparation." –Arthur Ashe

Writing a perfect résumé isn't overly difficult, but there is both art and science to it. If you ask ten recruiters what they want to see on a résumé, you'll get 15 different answers. There is no right or wrong way to write a résumé, but there are styles and functions that may work better for you as an individual. By reviewing examples and styles you can put together a document that works for you.

Your résumé is the first contact with a recruiter or hiring manager. You want to not only put your best foot forward but to also convince the reader that they need to call you.

Without one specific and clear set of rules for résumé writing it can be difficult for job seekers to know what to include and what to leave out. The suggestions in this book are not the only ways to design a résumé. I encourage you to use this information, your experiences, and feedback from others to craft a résumé that is personalized for you.

Don't forget to review, proofread, and edit your résumé to make sure it isn't being submitted with any spelling or grammatical errors. It is helpful to have a friend or family member look it over and provide a second pair of eyes. It may also be useful to read it out loud.

Types of Résumés

In general, résumés usually fall within one of three categories:

- *The Chronological Résumé*
- *The Functional Résumé*
- *The Hybrid Résumé*

> **The Chronological Résumé**
>
> This is the most common style of résumé. It typically features a list of jobs starting with the most recent and working backward. Here is an example:

Susan Smith

Address
Phone #   Email
LinkedIn Link
www.website.com

EXPERIENCE

Dates   Magazine   City, State

General Office Support

- Assisted the owner, publisher, and office manager with any tasks to help the publication occur smoothly.
- Created a catalog system for hundreds of manuals.
- Lead the marketing campaign for the 2013 edition of the *Buyer's Guide*, an industry publication of prominent related manufacturers around the world.

Dates   Staffing Company   City, State

Operations and Recruiting Specialist

- Specialized in the recruitment and placement of administrative professionals of all levels.
- Managed the company's internet presence.

- Processed all pre-employment screening with a variety of web sources for background checks, drug screens, and skills testing.
- Submitted all unemployment claims and participated in hearings as needed. Never lost a company-initiated appeal.
- Rewarded with a raise in salary and commission percentage even at a time of economic difficulty.

Dates   Direct Sales Company   City, State

Staffing Manager

- Responsible for all recruiting of national roster of field marketing representatives.
- Implemented a quality control program to ensure the continued success of our marketing programs.
- Developed an on-line application and employment qualification quiz from the ground up.

EDUCATION
University   City, State

Bachelor's Degree

Please note that in a real résumé all company names, city information, and dates will be complete and appropriate to the job seeker's individual experience.

> **The Functional Résumé**
>
> This style is popular among recent college graduates or individuals looking to change their careers. The idea is to showcase specific skills or accomplishments especially if the seeker doesn't have much experience.

SUSAN SMITH, PHR
email
Phone #
LinkedIn Profile

CREATIVE AND INTUITIVE HUMAN RESOURCES EXECUTIVE

VP OF HUMAN RESOURCES AT COMPANY NAME

While working my way into an executive position, I also pursued my passions of making a difference through volunteering, photography, and design.

PHR Certification Obtained 2012: Up to date with all current HR laws and regulations to ensure corporate compliance.

SKILLS

- Process Improvement
- Operations Management
- Problem Solving
- Team Building
- Employee Relations
- Coaching

- Hiring
- Manufacturing
- Mentoring
- Unemployment Hearings
- Worker's Compensation
- OSHA

ACCOMPLISHMENTS

Assisted in the growth of my organization from a $2 million company to over $35 million.

Company voted one of the best places to work in [My City] 2012.

Began career in design and trained with industrial and architectural designers before taking an interest in executive leadership. Experienced growth within the organization and enjoyed the increased responsibilities over time.

EXPERIENCE

Company Name *Dates*   *City, State*
Current Position: Vice President of Human Resources 2011-Present
Previously Held Positions: VP of HR and Business Development 2006-2011 and Designer 1994-2006

EDUCATION

Art Institute of City   Courses in commercial graphics
University   Bachelors of applied arts and sciences
PHR Certification (2012)

*Please note that in a real résumé all company names, city information, and dates will be complete and appropriate to the job seeker's individual experience.

Susan Smith

Address
Phone Number
Email

Objective

Currently seeking an administrative assistant position where my skills in organization and communication can be of service.

Accomplishments

Worked with the executive administrative assistant to arrange travel and calendars for the C-Level executives. Saved the company over $10,000 annually by establishing relationships with airlines, car rental services, and hotels.

Experience

Dates   Company   City, State

- Received a recommendation from the highest levels of the company as the administrative assistant of the year and provided an additional raise and bonus for my work.
- Utilized mobile technology to create a streamlined system for executive communication which saved the company $30,000 in the first year.

Dates   Company   City, State

- Promoted to lead administrative assistant after only six months on the job due to high praise from the corporate leadership.
- Worked with the pool of clerical professionals to streamline the data entry and file organization process in the entire office.

Education

University   City, State

Degree Obtained

Please note that in a real résumé all company names, city information, and dates will be complete and appropriate to the job seeker's individual experience.

Rule of Thumb

Your résumé only needs to go back ten years. Also, be sure to leave out any irrelevant experience such as work you did while in high school or college. The only exception should be more than ten continual years at the same job or experience that specifically relates to the job for which you're applying.

Your Contact Information

Most résumés will have your contact info at the top of the page. Depending on your preference, it can be justified to either margin, centered, or entered as a header. It is not recommended for you to get too fancy with this section. For most job seekers, use an easy-to-read font and simple black text on a white background. However, candidates in the creative and design fields can do more with their layout to showcase their skills.

So what do you need to include? A standard contact header includes your name, address, phone number, and email. You can leave your address off, but it is recommended, as many employers are looking for local candidates. A local phone number is not as important as it once was since so many people use cell phones exclusively. You may also want to include your web address and your LinkedIn profile URL.

If you are looking at a job in a different city from where you currently live it is recommended to use or borrow a local address. If you can't, this is a good reason to leave your address off all together. You can discuss relocation at a later step in the job search process.

If your résumé is two pages, you should include your name, number and email address at the bottom of the second page. That way if the pages do get separated they know where it belongs.

Rule of Thumb

How many pages should your résumé be? One or two pages are fine. A three page résumé is occasionally acceptable. Anything more should be cut for content. Remember: a résumé is an introduction, not a life story. More than three pages will most likely be discarded without being read.

The Objective

There is no more divisive concept in résumé writing than the objective statement. At one time the objective was considered essential to the résumé, but this is no longer the case.

Many recruiters suggest that you leave the objective off all together. If you skip this step you can avoid sending an "administrative assistant" résumé to a "graphic design" job. If you do choose to keep the objective, be diligent about editing it for every résumé you send out. Don't make your objective too general or hiring managers will be less likely to take you seriously. Since this is the first thing reviewers will see, it needs to be appropriate and to grab their attention.

When you write an objective, the statement should encompass your desired position, an accomplishment that makes you stand out, and a personal mission statement. Otherwise, you can skip this step.

For example:

Seeking an accounts payable/receivable position to apply my skills and further my career. Over ten years accounting assistant experience on multiple levels with consistent and reliable performance. Saved (Company Name) over $150,000 in 2013 by encouraging my contacts to pay their bills before they were past due.

How to Write a Cover Letter

In today's hyper-connected world, the cover letter is more important than ever. Emailing your résumé to a job posting without providing context for the reader is an exercise in futility. A cover letter gives you a platform to share details your résumé may not cover. This is, essentially, your sales pitch and is equally as important as your résumé.

Here are some easy-to-follow steps for writing a great cover letter:

- **Contact information:** In a formal letter you should have a header with your contact information just like your résumé, or include it in the top right-hand corner of the page. It is imperative that you have your name, phone number, and email address on every cover letter.
- **Salutation:** Before you compose the letter do as much research as you can to determine the recipient of the letter. This may be a recruiter, someone in human resources, or the hiring manager. Never open a letter with "To whom it may concern," as this will come across as impolite. If you cannot find the information anywhere on the job description, the company website, or LinkedIn, simply open the letter with "Good afternoon," or "Good morning."
- **Paragraph one:** A great cover letter follows a simple three paragraph format. The first paragraph should be a basic introduction. Don't start with "My name is," but rather reference the job posting. "I saw your listing for an executive administrative assistant, and I believe that my background is an excellent fit." Then go on to describe, in general terms, your qualifications.

- **Paragraph two:** The second paragraph should give the reader an idea of your accomplishments in this arena that are a match for their specific job. Review the job posting and determine the particular areas of concern or emphasis. Then match your experience with those and write about that. For example, "Over the last year, I created an office organizational system that eliminated most of our paper files and saved our company hours and money when it came to retaining and retrieving sensitive information regarding our clients."
- **Paragraph three:** Your final paragraph will let them know when you're available to interview, restate your interest in the job, and give them an idea of why you want to work for their company. "I am excited about the opportunity to work with a company that has a strong community service mindset and feel that my background and personal goals fit well within your organization." You should also make sure you include your contact information one more time in this paragraph. "You can reach me at (828) 555-5627 or email me at *my.name@internet.com*."

The Emailed Cover Letter

In most cases today your cover letter will not be mailed to the company but will be sent as an email with your résumé attached. You should still follow the same rules for composing this letter. However, you won't include your contact information at the top of the message. Instead, create a professional signature in your email client to appear at the end of the letter with your name, phone number, and email address. You can also include your LinkedIn profile link or a website.

How to Interview

"Whether you think you can or think you can't, you're right." –Henry Ford

They say you never get a second chance to make a first impression, and this has never been more true than in a job interview.

Your interview starts long before you set foot in the office and begin the conversation. Every step you take, from choosing your clothes to mapping your drive, is essential. You will also be judged by how you treat the receptionist and your telephone skills. Let's break down the interview into the basic parts.

Preparing for Your Interview

Once you've received a positive phone call as a result of your résumé, the work to impress the potential employer directly becomes essential. Your job is to not only prove that you're qualified but to also demonstrate that you're right for this company. Employers don't want to hire someone who just wants any job; they want to know that their new employee is dedicated to the company mission, is interested in the work, and is loyal to the organization. If you are not all of these things, the relationship simply won't work.

Of course, the ultimate goal of any job search should be to get the position you really want at a company you enjoy working for. Always keep these goals in mind when you're job searching.

- **Step 1: The Phone Interview**

Typically, before you meet with the hiring manager face-to-face you'll have a phone interview. You need to treat this conversation with as much importance as your first real meeting. Don't be late for the phone call, follow any directions provided, and go somewhere to talk where you will be uninterrupted. One of the biggest complaints from hiring managers is that far too many job seekers are distracted on the initial phone call. This is a red flag, and they will be looking for reasons to narrow down the field of candidates.

- **Step 2: Research the company**

You need to be as prepared as possible before you enter the meeting. The worst question you can ask is, "What does your company do?" You should already know this along with some basic, general information about the organization.

On the surface level, you should review the company website to get a better understanding of their message and how they brand themselves.

On a deeper level, check LinkedIn to look at others who have worked with the company before. Look at other social media accounts as well, such as the company Facebook page and Twitter.

Be prepared with intelligent questions that can help the company better understand you as a viable candidate. Ask them questions like:

- What can I expect to accomplish in my first month?
- What makes your employees successful?
- How does the company make money? What is my role in this process?
- What are the long-term plans for the company?

These questions will give the employer a sense of why you're looking to work with them and give them an opportunity to share more about their company mission and culture with you.

- **Step 3: Choose your clothing**

You want to make a good first impression and your clothes will dictate this for the employer.

Your clothing must be clean and wrinkle-free. You should also pay attention to your own hygiene on the day of the interview.

Keep your accessories to a minimum. They can become distracting if they are overwhelming. Also, never wear cologne or perfume to an interview because many people have allergies or sensitivities to scents.

For men, a suit and tie is still the best choice. You can skip the suit jacket and just wear a button-down shirt with a tie if that is more comfortable.

For women, a tailored suit with either pants or a skirt is appropriate. Keep away from wild colors and try to choose something more conservative.

If the company is more creative you can choose fun accessories or colors.

Have you heard of the capsule wardrobe? This is an idea many women are picking up in the business world. It is based on the idea that most men don't spend a lot of time worrying about the clothes they wear since slacks and shirts prevail in the office culture. A female capsule wardrobe is enough of the same shirt and pants or skirts to wear them every day and not feel fashion pressure. It is a great way to stay professional and focus on your work rather than your clothes.

Rule of Thumb

What do you do if the employer tells you to dress casually for the interview? Some businesses have a very casual environment and will instruct interviewers to wear jeans or other casual clothes. It may be a test to see how well you follow directions so listen to them and plan accordingly. Even if you wear jeans, make sure your clothing isn't sloppy or dirty. Wear appropriately tailored jeans and a professional shirt. Never wear a t-shirt with logos or other screen printing.

- **Step 4: Plan your Route**

The worst thing you can do on the day of your interview is be late. This sets the tone not only for the interview itself but you as an employee. If you set the precedent that you are likely to be late to work regularly, they may not make an offer at all.

When you're confirming your interview ask for directions. Ask if Google maps or GPS is usually accurate to their location. GPS is much better today than it was even a few years ago, so more people are relying on it. However, it isn't always perfect, and you need to be aware of potential issues.

If you can, make a trial run to the site. Learn the best route, and see how long it takes. Factor in traffic or other challenges on the road, such as construction, and make a plan to avoid that. Try the drive in rush hour traffic as well to see what the commute will be like if you accept the job.

On the day of the interview, have the company phone number available. Emergencies do happen, so as soon as you realize you're running late call and let them know.

Plan to arrive on site about ten to fifteen minutes early for your appointment.

- **Step 5: Treat the Receptionist Well**

An interview starts long before shaking hands with the hiring manager. One of the first things they'll check into after you've left is what the receptionist thought of you. You may be surprised to learn that some candidates are less than polite to the person managing the front of the office.

Introduce yourself, and offer to shake hands. Let them know who you're there to meet and when your appointment is scheduled.

Once you're checked in you can have a seat. If the receptionist is busy, respect their time and wait in silence. However, if you gauge the situation and determine that you might be able to ask a few questions that is also appropriate. This will depend largely on the situation. If the receptionist does not appear receptive to your questions, don't continue.

Always thank them on your way out.

- **Step 6: Know Your Body Language**

Once you are called back for the interview, pay specific attention to your body language. The words you say are important, but the way you say them is also critical. Make sure your handshake is firm. Make appropriate eye contact.

Another great technique is mirroring. This is where you subtly let your body language reflect that of the speaker. It connects you and makes them more at east.

Be careful not to use body language that communicates dominance. This is especially important for men who are interviewing with women. Spreading your arms or legs can be viewed negatively.

- **Step 7: Know What Questions to Answer**

Not every interviewer is skilled at the art of interviewing. Unfortunately, a few of them are likely to ask inappropriate questions. They may ask things that are too personal or questions that are prohibited by law. How do you handle this?

You do not need to answer any questions about your age, your marital status, children, religion, disability, or sexual orientation. If you are asked something about these subjects, the best way to handle it is to simply decline and redirect.

For example:

Interviewer: "Do you have children in school activities?"

You: "I will have no problem working the hours expected."

- **Step 8: Ask Questions**

You should also have some questions in mind to ask the interviewer. This demonstrates to the hiring manager that you've done your homework and that you're excited about the opportunity.

In truth, the interviewer may answer some of your prepared questions in the course of the conversation, so have some subjects in mind along the way. Good subjects include:

- Tell me more about the corporate environment and culture.
- What is the manager like in the department? What would help me fit in well with coworkers there?
- What is your favorite part about working for this company?

Rule of Thumb

When should you ask about the next step in the process? Never leave an interview without asking when they plan to make a decision. This will give you a timeframe for following up. Don't forget to take their business card.

How to Follow Up

"When it is obvious that the goals cannot be reached, don't adjust the goals, adjust the action steps." –Confucius

Far too many job seekers believe that their work is done after the interview. The employer needs to make the decision now, so the ball is in their court now, right?

There are some things you can do after the interview to impress the hiring managers even more, and if you are one of the few job seekers who takes these steps it will only enhance your position.

Send a Thank You Note

As soon as you get home from the interview the first thing you should do is send a thank you note.

There are two schools of thought when it comes to this added touch, and neither are wrong.

- **Option One: Send an Email**

The corporate environment is highly digitalized, so companies expect a lot of communications to come via email. The major benefit of this is it will happen much more quickly than a mailed note.

Compose an email that recaps your conversation, reiterates your interest, and even touches on things you forgot to mention. You now have a second opportunity to make an impression.

For Example:

Dear Emily,

Thank you so much for taking the time to meet with me this morning. I am very excited about the potential opportunity to work with Intrepid Corp.

As we discussed, I feel that my experience with accounts receivable mirrors the processes your company already uses. It won't take long for me to learn any specifics from your already great team.

I forgot to mention that I also have experience with making collections calls. If there is a skipped invoice I have no problem contacting the company to determine the issue in the most efficient and effective way possible. I know collections can be challenging for some people, but I am very comfortable on the phone.

I look forward to speaking with you again. Feel free to contact me via email or call (404) 555-9284.

Thank you,
Frances

Be sure to restate your contact information to make it as easy as possible to hit reply or pick up the phone.

- **Option 2: Send a Thank You Note**

Some people prefer the more personal option of sending a hand-written thank you note. This can be on branded stationary or a simple card. The general concept is to thank the interviewer for taking the time to meet you and to let them know you look forward to the next conversation.

A formal thank you note doesn't have to include too many details about the interview itself as it will be received several days after the interview. Be complimentary about the things you enjoyed from the interview or the company.

Rule of Thumb

There is no rule that says you can't send both types of thank you notes. Since the each serve a different basic purpose you can send an email right away that recaps your conversation and shares information you forgot to mention. At the same time, send a hand-written thank you in the mail. They will get both and think positively about you as a candidate while they're making a decision.

Checking On the Status of the Job

During the interview you asked what the next steps would be. In their answer the interviewer probably gave you an indication of their timeframe to make a decision.

If they did not give you a specific timeframe, the accepted wait time is a week after the interview.

When you do follow up, it is important to not come across as pushy or demanding. The hiring manager has a lot of roles within the company, not just interviewing. They may have other priorities that are taking up their time. Be polite and professional throughout your communications.

You can either send a follow up email or make a phone call. An email gives them an opportunity to respond when their schedule allows. If you do call them, try to plan your call time between 10 a.m. and noon. It allows them to have completed their urgent work for the morning, but it is before their lunch hour.

How to Negotiate Salary

"Money is a guarantee that we may have what we want in the future. Though we need nothing at the moment it insures the possibility of satisfying a new desire when it arises." –Aristotle

The original vision of this book ended after the section on following up. Then, when several friends began talking to me about changing jobs, I realized that few people really understood the complications of negotiating a salary.

In fact, most professionals are taught to avoid salary negotiations at all cost. We're told that the company has a budget, and they will make the offer, but this isn't entirely true. A negotiation should be a conversation. Both parties should have enough knowledge of the market in the area to speak intelligently about money.

Money is a complicated issue. It can also be an emotional one. Sometimes we can't separate these feelings from what they represent. The one time it is most important is when you're talking to a potential employer about salary.

When is it appropriate to discuss?

There was saying among staffing professionals: "The first person to say a number loses."

That is far too simplistic a statement. A healthy negotiation takes work, but there are times when discussing money is inappropriate.

During a phone interview, for instance, the recruiter or hiring manager may ask how much you want to make. They're trying to rule people out at this point, so if you say more than they're planning to pay they will place your résumé in the "No" pile. If you say significantly less, they may be intrigued because they can get away with paying you under their budget.

You should never answer this question in a phone interview. Instead, focus on the job and skill necessary, and let them know that you're within the salary range.

If you are asked about salary on the phone, suggest that you would like to research the position and the company further before discussing money.

The best time to discuss money is after the first interview or as a part of the second interview process.

What do you want?

So how much should you ask for? This, of course, depends on a number of factors. You should do your research to find out what similar positions in your area are paying. The best resource for this is www.salary.com.

The important thing you need to know is that your current salary has absolutely no bearing on what your future position should pay. Many recruiters and hiring managers will automatically ask you for a salary history, but it is perfectly acceptable to withhold this information.

Your current salary or what your current company pays should not influence the salary that you negotiate and accept for a future position. Instead, base your numbers on your research.

How do you avoid providing this information? Say something like, "I've done research on the salary for this type of position in our city and (salary amount) is within the range." You still give them a figure they can work with, but you don't disclose your current salary.

Rule of Thumb

You never have to accept an offer on the spot. Let the job interviewer know that you need to review the numbers they've provided and get back to them with your answer. This is a good time to review Salary.com.

Walk-away number

Your negotiations should always start with a range. Chances are the company shared a range with their original job posting, so that is a good place to begin. Once you research what the type of position pays on average in your city you can create a strategy that plays up your strengths.

You should always have a "walk-away" number in mind when you're negotiating. This is the lowest possible salary you will accept and still be able to pay your bills and contribute to your savings. Once you have this number in mind, know that no matter what the company or job is, you need to respectfully decline an offer for less than your walk-away number. This can also kick-start new negotiations. If you share that their offer simply doesn't work for you they may ask what would work.

The most important thing to keep in mind is that you need to remain confident, but not arrogant, during negotiations. You are worth the salary you've asked for provided you're not reaching beyond the normal range for the job and the area.

Starting Your New Job

"The best preparation for good work tomorrow is to do good work today." –Elbert Hubbard

Some final thoughts for you as you continue on your job search.

When you do start a job, go in prepared. Don't be afraid to try new things or ask for new responsibilities. If you don't feel connected to the company or the work you're doing, it may not be the right fit for you. Spending more time on your job search can help you find work that is meaningful to you.

Do these four things to start your new job off with success:

1. **Introduce yourself.** Meet other people in your office. Not just your immediate coworkers, but take time to say hi to everyone you come in contact with. You never know who can help you out down the road or who might turn into a trusted colleague.

2. **Find a mentor.** Someone in your office has a lot of offer. When you choose a mentor you are opening yourself up to learning opportunities. A mentor can help you learn from their mistakes, function as a sounding board, and provide motivation when you need it most.

3. **Don't go through the motions.** Work hard from day one. There will always be a learning curve, so do you best to get past it quickly. Take notes, ask questions, and try everything with enthusiasm. Hard work will always get more recognition than just showing up.

4. **Communicate.** When you don't know something, ask. When you don't know who to ask, find out. When you have a concern, say something. When someone helps you out, thank them. The more you communicate with others the more others will communicate with you.

Best of luck in your new job!

Acknowledgements

After 15 years in recruiting I did something absolutely terrifying: I quit my job. I jumped head first into freelance writing without a safety net and I am grateful for everyone who helped me along the way.

Thanks to the team at my previous recruiting jobs. Eight of those years were with a great group of people near Atlanta, Georgia.

Thanks to the marketing group that took a chance on me as a novice writer and gave me an opportunity to contribute blog posts for a variety of staffing clients about topics just like the ones presented in this book.

Thanks to my mentors and accountability groups. Everyone who has helped keep me going is a superstar in by book. Especially Suzannah Kolbeck, who helped me with final edits.

Finally, thanks to my partner in life since 1995. We've taken some crazy chances, and I don't think we would have been half as successful if we weren't a team.

www.ingramcontent.com/pod-product-compliance
Lightning Source LLC
Chambersburg PA
CBHW071003180526
45168CB00003B/1274